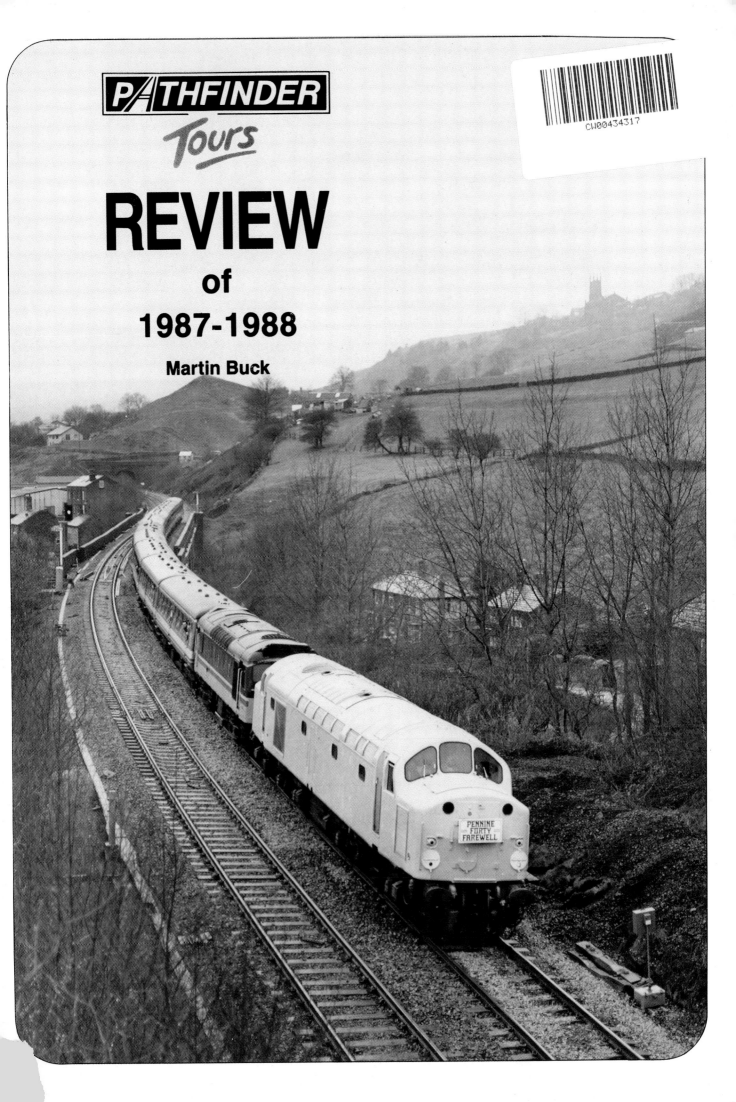

PATHFINDER Tours

REVIEW
of
1987-1988

Martin Buck

Front Cover:
The theme behind the photographs on the front cover is to depict the main types of locomotives which have appeared on the majority of Pathfinder charters during 1987/88 viz. Classes 45, 37, 50 and steam locomotives. *all Martin Buck*

Frontispiece:
This photograph is of a very unique Pathfinder charter – the 'Pennine Forty Farewell' and shows D200 + Ethel 3 between Castle Hill and Horsefall Tunnels, Todmorden, running over 1½ hours late. *A.J. Woof*

Back Cover:
This shows D200 at Oakdale Colliery during run-round manoeuvres on the May 23rd 1987, 'Gwent Valley Explorer'. *Steve Widdowson*

Below: The 'Yorkshire Venturer' is seen at Scarborough on August 7th 1988, with 2-10-0 'Evening Star' ready to depart for Hull. *Bert Wynn*

© COPYRIGHT 1989
Published by: Pathfinder Tours, Stag House, Gydynap Lane, Inchbrook
Woodchester, Nr. Stroud, Gloucestershire, GL5 5EZ.

ISBN 0 906025 37 0
Cover: Originated by Radstock Reproduction, Midsomer Norton and printed by Pheon Press, Bristol.
Text: Typeset and printed by W.B.C. Print, Bristol
Bound by W.H. Ware, Clevedon.

Introduction

PATHFINDER TOURS was launched on January 1st 1987, under the Directorship of Martin Buck and Peter Watts, with the intention of establishing the Company as a dominant force in the charter train market.

With many rail enthusiasts in the country we realised that there was a definite need for a programme of special trains incorporating the various interests within the movement, such as freight line travel and steam/diesel haulage, for example. There was also a further demand, especially from the general public, for special trains over scenic routes and to interesting destinations.

So, with this in mind, we embarked on a wide programme of special trains to cater for, primarily, the people living in the Mid-West, Severnside and West Midlands area of the country. Of course, as our product became known and established, people living in other areas travelled to join our tours, from as far and wide as Penzance, Dover and Edinburgh, which gives you an idea of the widespread appeal of *Pathfinder Tours.*

Now, two years later and with approaching 40 special trains under our belt, we feel the time is right to look back and 'Review' our 1987–1988 operation. The main reasons for doing this are to provide our passengers with a comprehensive, illustrated record of all the special trains on which they may have participated and to reflect on how the charter train scene has changed and will change in the future.

All the special trains covered in this title are, what I would class as, 'railtours' because they include a combination of features – haulage behind specific motive power, travel over scenic routes/freight lines and offer optional activities for passengers, which are sacrosanct with such a tour. For this reason, the October 17 1987, 'Blackpool Illuminator', charter from Bristol to Blackpool, has not been included because it was merely an excursion, containing none of the above mentioned features.

As a charter train operator, we endeavoured to provide interesting and unusual tours, which featured, for example, taking certain classes of locomotive to unfamiliar territory. It may well be that we achieved many 'firsts', such as the visit of 45110 to Fishguard Harbour but, as this would involve extensive research and might be difficult to substantiate, I will leave this aspect for you to decide.

The 'On-Train' service is also an important aspect of a 'railtour' and we have provided a wide range of services to our passengers, which we consider essential. These include, friendly and helpful coach stewards, catering facilities, sales-stand and a raffle in aid of a recognised charity or transport preservation group. Many people and organisations have assisted in providing these services and, as they are too numerous to mention individually, I would like to extend my thanks to them collectively for their help and dedication.

Pathfinder Tours, not unlike any other business, has experienced its share of problems and disappointments, many of which affect you, our passengers. These include, for example, those railtours which were advertised in good faith and bookings received for but, late in the day, had to be cancelled due to operational difficulties beyond our control – like the proposed 'Southern Vectis Venturer' and 'Class 27' railtours in 1987.

We have established a good working relationship with British Rail – the Inter-City Charter Train Unit, based in London, with whom we initially liaise to confirm our proposals and agree the charter fees and the B.R. 'originating' Region for a tour, with whom we co-ordinate the details and check progress. This, in effect, is our main channel of communication in planning tours and if we receive charter train information from them quickly and precisely, we can provide you with a first class and efficient service.

It is true to say that the charter train operation has had to change by decree over the last two years and, if *Pathfinder Tours* was to remain a viable operation, it was also important that we too changed our approach and adopted the new guidelines laid down by British Rail. Well, what were the changes? . . .

Basically, the main change concerned motive power. During 1987, we could request the majority of passenger rated and 'Railfreight' locomotives to haul our trains but, from January 1988, the rules changed and 'Railfreight' locomotives became unavailable to haul charter trains. This decision may seem rather ironic to many people, if you consider that such locomotives were regularly diagrammed to work certain 'Summer Dated' passenger services on B.R., like class 20 and 37 locomotives on the Skegness and Cambrian routes, respectively, in particular. Whilst this apparent anomaly remains, it can do nothing but cause confusion and disappointment to the railtouring public.

From January 1989, the rules and guidelines change again in that 'requested' motive power should be restricted to the use of 45106 (later changed to 45128) and 37350, when diesel hauled charters are concerned – if these two are unacceptable, then haulage must be behind the ubiquitous class 47 locomotive. We must, therefore, wait and see how this situation develops.

Additionally, there is the problem of route availability, which is restricted to train driver traction and route knowledge, thus reducing the costly need of pilotmen. A further factor is increasing charter fees, which can be prohibitive and restrictive, especially on long distance tours and we may see the 'Son O' Skirl' type tour becoming a thing of the past.

It is for this reason, we ran the 'Pennine Executives', late in 1988, to test the market for luxury dining trains, to see if these could supplement a conventional railtour programme, in the light of these new changes. I am pleased to say they were a total success and we see these dining trains becoming the core of our business, plus a number of selected diesel and steam hauled special trains, in 1989 and beyond.

At this stage, I would like to state a few statistics for 1987 and 1988, which I hope will provide additional information about *Pathfinder Tours*. A full list of the locomotives which have featured on our tours is given in the 'Glossary' towards the back of this title.

- Number of trains run : 39 (inclusive of 1 BR re-run)
- Geographical rail miles covered : 27,000 plus
  - minimum mileage : 438 on 'Rheidol Rambler'
  - maximum mileage : 1,934 on 'Caledonian'
  - average mileage : 695 per tour
- Number of locomotives featured : 148 (excluding 'Ethels')
  - maximum number : 13 on 'Son O' Skirl'
- Number of passengers conveyed : 12,800 in total
  - new passengers : 2,900 (23%)

Finally, I would like to acknowledge my thanks to all the photographers who kindly submitted material for consideration in this title. It has certainly been both a privilege and pleasure for me to compile 'PATHFINDER TOURS REVIEW of 1987–1988', which I hope will rekindle fond memories of your travel with Pathfinder Tours.

Swindon
Wiltshire
January 1989

Martin Buck
Director

1987

March 7th:
CUMBRIAN MOUNTAINEER

The inaugural Pathfinder tour ran on March 7th from Plymouth to Carlisle. A circular route from Birmingham was involved taking in Ais Gill on the outward journey and Shap on the return. A Class 45/1 locomotive was the featured motive power.

The tour left Bristol T.M. hauled by 45120, which was subsequently declared a failure at Derby. Luckily, B.R. managed to replace it there with another 'Peak', 45119, which took the tour forward and back to Bristol T.M. in the evening, where it was replaced.

The two photographs show the 'Cumbrian Mountaineer' during a photostop at Garsdale in wintry conditions. In fact, on leaving Carlisle the weather quickly deteriorated and the journey over Shap was made in a blizzard with visibility being nil through the carriage window. The *top* photograph shows Company Directors Martin Buck *(left)* and Peter Watts *(right)* looking and feeling decidedly cold!

Bert Wynn/Norman Preedy

March 21st: YORKSHIRE ROSE

During the winter timetable (October–May) a passenger train must be hauled by an engine capable of providing train-heat and to give variety a Class 37/4 was requested for our railtour to York. We chose a circular route and travelled outward via Stockport, the Calder Valley, Healey Mills and Harrogate and returned from York via Knottingley, Doncaster and Toton. At Doncaster we experienced train crew difficulties as the rostered guard did not turn up. The existing guard was only prepared to work the train as far as Toton, where we had to wait a considerable amount of time until a new guard could be driven in by taxi from Derby.

The photographs show 37430 heading through Sowerby Bridge *(above)* on the Calder Valley line and approaching Holgate Junction *(below)*, after leaving York.

Pathfinder Tours/N.E. Stead

April 18th:
TAMAR FORTH EXPRESS

I would like to comment on B.R. Charter Train c[...]
as they do have a bearing on this tour. Normally, [...]
fee includes a charge for each locomotive request[...]
which reduces if no motive power is selected. Thus,[...]
advertised the 'Tamar Forth Express' as a railtou[...]
Edinburgh, featuring optional activities for passeng[...]
at our destination but, without specified traction. B[...]
would provide either a through-diesel or interchang[...]
with a 25 KV Electric locomotive over the electrif[...]
section of the route.

As it turned out, 8 locomotives featured on the t[...]
which, had they been requested, would have cos[...]
significant amount of money. The highlight for ma[...]
passengers was the pair of Class 26 locomoti[...]
between Carstairs–Edinburgh–Carstairs. Ironica[...]
when we requested Class 26's for the later 'Son [...]
Skirl' and 'Caledonian' railtours, B.R. could [...]
provide them!

The 'Tamar Forth Express' is the only Pathfin[...]
Tour to ever feature Class 26 locomotives, so I thoug[...]
it only appropriate to reproduce photographs wh[...]
illustrate them. The pair (26032 + 26043) are seen [...]
Carstairs *(top/middle)* on the outward journey and [...]
Edinburgh *(bottom)* bringing the e.c.s. into Waver[...]
station. *Norman Preedy (2)/Bert Wy[...]*

May 3rd: HASTINGS BELLE

This landcruise travelled through the heart of Sussex to East Grinstead and the coastal towns of Hastings and Eastbourne, featuring Class 56 haulage for the majority of the day. As an option, passengers had the opportunity to visit the Bluebell Railway whilst the tour journied between East Grinstead and Eastbourne.

Our ultimate destination was Eastbourne where, upon arrival, the heavens opened up and we experienced a severe hail storm. A Class 73 locomotive worked the train between Eastbourne and Hastings and the photographs show the 'Hastings Belle' at these two stations. At Hastings, under a threatening stormy sky, 56033 *(above)* was coupled to the train for the journey to Paddington, where it was replaced by 56048 for the final leg to Bristol. At Eastbourne, 73132 *(below)* awaits the departure time of 15.34 for its 15½ mile run to Hastings.

Norman Preedy/Bert Wynn

May 23rd: GWENT VALLEY EXPLORER

The 'Gwent Valley Explorer' entailed a visit to the valleys of South Wales, where snaking freight lines penetrate deep amongst the hills. On this occasion, we concentrated on three lines radiating from Newport – to Waunllwyd (Ebbw Vale), Machen and Oakdale, plus the short spur from Barry to Barry Island. To add extra interest, we featured D200 as prime motive power, with the highlight being the run to Oakdale Colliery, which certainly provided a challenge to the locomotive. Whilst D200 was being serviced at Cardiff Canton, 37220 worked the train to Machen and 37280 to Barry Island.

The photographs show the tour at three destinations. At Barry Island *(above)*, 37280 ran round the stock and gave our passengers the opportunity to stretch their legs before leaving for Cardiff. The 'whistler' is seen at Waunllwyd *(right upper)* the location of the BSC tinplate works, which processes hot rolled coil from Ravenscraig, Llanwern and Margam. On the final leg of the journey 40122 is seen waiting to leave Oakdale Colliery *(right lower)*, for the six hour run back to Crewe. *Steve Widdowson/B.G. Hughes/Norman Preedy*

May 31st: BARMOUTH BAY EXPRESS

1967 saw the running of the last steam hauled passenger train over the former Cambrian Railways system through mid-Wales and along the scenic coast line to Portmadoc and it was appropriate, twenty years on, that steam traction returned to its former haunts. B.R. organised special steam runs between Machynlleth and Barmouth using either the ex-GWR 'Manor' Class 4-6-0 no. 7819 'Hinton Manor' or Standard 4MT Class 4-6-0 no. 75069. We decided to run a special train to Machynlleth to feed in to the steam operation and for this purpose we hired the privately owned 'Pullman-Rail', maroon liveried, stock.

Between Bristol and Machynlleth a pair of Class 37 locomotives worked the train and 37159 + 37204 are seen leaving Gloucester *(above)* and passing Wadborough *(below)*, as they approach Worcester Shrub Hill, on the outward journey. *Barry Nicolle/Steve Widdowson*

We travelled via Shrewsbury, Welshpool and the Upper Severn Valley before climbing over the Cambrian Hills and down into the Dovey Valley and Machynlleth. A stop for pathing requirements at Newtown gave passengers the opportunity to photograph 37159 + 37204 (above) before proceeding further.

At Machynlleth, passengers transferred to B.R.'s 1L40, 1445 Machynlleth–Barmouth steam service, made up of chocolate and cream coaches, hauled by 7819 'Hinton Manor'. On a glorious sunny day, we had a wonderful ride along the Dovey Estuary and over the scenic Cambrian Coast Line to Barmouth, entering via the world famous bridge across the Mawddach Estuary. A short break was had at Barmouth, during which time the photographer captured 7819 (below), sporting a 'Cambrian Coast Express' headboard.

Both Norman Preedy

June 27th:
AINTREE HURDLER

Class 58 'Railfreight' locomotives rarely have the opportunity to haul passenger trains, especially over substantial distances, so for June 27th we decided to feature this class. This particular rail cruise covered a good cross section of the English countryside, from the Welsh Marches to the Pennines and Derbyshire Dales. The highlight being traversal of the 'threatened with closure' route through the suburbs of Liverpool to Aintree.

Our first Class 58 locomotive came on at Shrewsbury and 58042 is seen leaving the market town of Shrewsbury *(above)* and approaching the outskirts of the City of Chester *(left)* on the outward journey.

The return journey from Aintree was via the 'Oldham Loop', Hope Valley and Toton, where 58042 was substituted for 58031. On the *opposite* page, 58042 is seen about to leave Aintree *(right upper)* and traversing the single track 'Oldham Loop' at Shaw *(right lower)*, near Oldham.

At the end of the day, passengers had enjoyed 268 miles haulage behind Class 58 locomotives. *Peter Tandy/B.G. Hughes and Norman Preedy/Mike Taylor*

July 12th: WELSH RAMBLER

The Central Wales line is one of the Principality's most scenic routes and over its 90 mile route length, it ambles along river valley, climbs over hill and dale, linking small hamlets from Llanelli to Craven Arms. This was the destination of the 'Welsh Rambler' and we featured 2 × Class 20 locomotives as motive power. These worked throughout until Birmingham in the evening except, between Margam and Swansea, when they were being refuelled.

We decided to include an optional 'traditional roast lunch', so passengers did not have to go without their Sunday roast! This aspect of the tour was publicised and it appealed to the general public, proving that 'dining' trains could be an attractive proposition. In fact, 35% of the passengers on board the 'Welsh Rambler', were travelling with *Pathfinder Tours* for the first time – tempted by the dining option.

The pictures show 20021 + 20113 at Carmarthen *(above)* during the morning break and at Craven Arms *(below)* during a photo-stop.

Bert Wynn/Norman Preedy

July 25th:
HUMBERMAN

Pathfinder Tours endeavour to run a Summer 'Spotters Special' once a year and 1987 was no exception, with the 'Humberman' fitting the bill. Once everyone was aboard, we headed to South Yorkshire and Humberside, passing many well known loco. holding points such as Saltley, Toton, Tinsley, Doncaster and Immingham.

Two Class 37 locomotives were the advertised motive power with the highlight for many passengers being traversal of the 'freight only' Immingham Loop. As an alternative for those who did not want to travel over this section of line, an optional visit to Immingham T.M.P.D. was laid on for a modest fee of £2.50, which covered the cost of permits and coach transfer to and from the tour.

The 'Humberman' is seen heading into South Yorkshire at Chesterfield *(top)* with 37699 + 37139 in charge. The tour then ran to Doncaster Decoy Yard *(middle)* to enable the 37's to run round for the journey into Humberside. At Cleethorpes, it is not possible to release a locomotive from the stock so at Barnetby our 37's came off and ran 'light' to Cleethorpes for the return journey. At Barnetby *(bottom)*, 47222 came on for the short stretch to Cleethorpes.

N.E. Stead/Norman Preedy (2)

August 9th: RHEIDOL RAMBLER

The Cambrian Coast area of Wales is always a popular destination for a day out and Aberystwyth was our destination on this occasion. Initially, the tour was advertised to feature haulage over the Cambrian Coast line behind a single Class 20 locomotive but, unfortunately, B.R. insisted that two of these engines must work the train.

Passengers had the option of either travelling to Aberystwyth, for a steam run on the narrow gauge Vale of Rheidol railway, or to alight at Machynlleth and connect into the special B.R. 'Cardigan Bay Express' steam run from Machynlleth to Pwllheli and return.

The Class 20 locomotives, 20034 + 20133, were diagrammed to work the Wolverhampton–Aberystwyth–Wolverhampton section of the tour and are seen stabled at Aberystwyth *(above)* during the 5¾ hour lay-over at our destination. It would appear that time has stood still on at least two occasions, if the station clocks are anything to go by!

Steve Widdowson

August 22nd: NORTHUMBRIAN

The 'Northumbrian' was *Pathfinder Tours* first trip to the North-East of England, with access to and from Newcastle being planned via York and the E.C.M.L. However, due to extensive engineering work in the North-East it was necessary to re-route the train via Carlisle, travelling by way of the S. & C. on the outward journey and Shap on the return. This was a real bonus to passengers, providing rare Class 56 haulage over these two classic routes.

The tour got off to an awful start because the stock was failed at Swindon due to defective train-lights in some of the coaches. Passengers had to wait for well over an hour before a replacement set of coaches arrived at Swindon. This new set had been commandeered at Didcot, whilst working a Manchester-Paddington express, with the passengers being transferred to another service.

Our first Class 56 (56016) came on at New St. Station for the Birmingham–Carlisle–Birmingham section of the tour. The run from Carlisle to, and back from, Newcastle involved 37180, which handed over to 56005 at the latter point for a journey round the Morpeth Loop. The pictorial record of the 'Northumbrian' is at Newcastle, showing 37180 *(right)* stabled in between turns and 56005 *(below)* waiting to hand over to the 37 during a downpour.

both Steve Turner

September 18-20th: SON O' SKIRL

Our weekend visit to the rugged West Coast of Scotland featured a mixture of diesel and steam locomotives. We advertised motive power in Scotland as 2 × Class 26 locomotives but, unfortunately, shortly before the tour was due to run, B.R. informed us that 26's could not be provided.

On the outward Journey from Carlisle we featured D200 for a northbound run over Beattock to Mossend, where we exchanged D200 for a pair of 37's for the journey to Fort William. Between Arrochar and Crianlarich, the locomotives struggled to find power and we wondered if we were going to make Crianlarich. The 37's, 37092 + 37043, are seen leaving Bridge of Orchy *(above)* heading for Rannoch and, ultimately, Fort William, where passengers transferred to a special steam train, which we had exclusively hired for the day. The featured locomotive was K1 2-6-0 no. 2005 and this is seen at Pulnoch *(below)* heading for the fishing port of Mallaig.   *both Gavin Morrison*

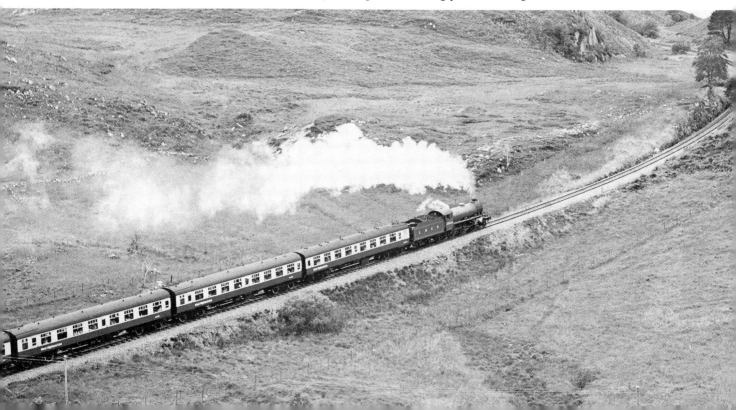

The 'K1' is seen at Arisaig station *(above)* with passengers making their way back to the coaches after a photostop. Back at Fort William, we transferred to the main train and headed south for an evening break in Glasgow. As an optional activity, the majority of passengers alighted at Arrochar for a cruise down Loch Lomond to Balloch Pier in m.v. 'Countess Fiona'. In fact, due to the demand, a second boat was laid on. From Balloch Pier passengers travelled by service train to Glasgow Central to rejoin the tour.

We travelled overnight to Manchester Victoria behind D200 over Beattock and Shap to join a special sunday morning steam run from Manchester to Southport hauled by A3 4-6-2 No. 4472 'Flying Scotsman', which is seen at Victoria *(below)* prior to working the train. After a break in Southport, we rejoined our train for a run to Gloucester behind 20052 + 20104. Unfortunately, 20104 failed at Penkridge, and 20154 + 20197 came on at Bescot to complete the run to Gloucester.

both Steve Widdowson

October 3rd: 45 FINALE

The confirmed withdrawal date for the remaining 'Peak' class locomotives was set for the weekend of October 3/4. With this in mind, we organised a special, circular, 'Farewell' tour involving, not one but, two class members at the head of the train for most of the day and gave passengers a special certificate to commemorate this event. Not surprisingly, the '45 Finale' proved to be our best supported train during 1987 even though, as it turned out, the 45's were not withdrawn from service that weekend.

From Birmingham New Street, the tour was headed by 45007 + 45106 but, due to engine failure, 45106 was taken off at Leicester and replaced by 45107. The new pair, 45007 + 45107, are seen passing through Chesterfield *(above)* and at Weaverthorpe *(below)*, between Malton and Scarborough, on the outward journey.

N.E. Stead/B.G. Hughes

A short break was taken at Scarborough to enable the 45's to 'run round' before proceeding to Hull. The route to Hull is mostly single track and 45107 + 45007 are seen on such a section at Bartindale *(above)*, south of Hunmanby. On arrival at Hull, the locomotives were refuelled and the stock watered before leaving for home by way of Boothferry Park and Knottingley East & South Junctions, which were included to provide further interest. The charter, 1Z46, is seen departing from Hull Paragon station *(below)*, in a photograph which clearly shows the extent of the former station layout.   *both N.E. Stead*

October 31st: SEVERN CLYDE EXPRESS

In response to many requests, we presented this day tour to the hub of Scotland, the City of Glasgow, and offered passengers a range of optional activities to choose from. These included: *(i)* a visit to B.R. depots at Ayr, Eastfield and Yoker, *(ii)* a coach tour of historic Glasgow or, *(iii)* a coach tour to the beautiful Trossachs – in fact, probably something for everyone!

We had a spirited run up the W.C.M.L. behind 87029, which was replaced at Carlisle by a Class 47 locomotive and 47653 is seen at Citadel station *(above)* ready to leave for the journey to Glasgow Central, over the ex-G.S.W. route via Dumfries, the Drumlanrig Gorge and Kilmarnock. On the return journey, a pair of Class 20 locomotives worked the train to Carstairs and 20205 + 20217 are seen at Glasgow Central *(below)* prior to departure.   *both Norman Preedy*

November 14th: SKIPTON SKIPPER

This tour presented passengers with the rare opportunity of travelling behind a Class 50 locomotive over lines in the old West Riding of Yorkshire. We chose a circular route via Penistone, Healey Mills and Leeds, traversing both the Ilkley and Bradford Forster Square branches en-route to Keighley and Skipton. An optional break was taken at Keighley, where passengers had the opportunity of making an exclusive return journey to Oxenhope on the Keighley & Worth Valley Railway.

The 'Skipton Skipper' certainly captured the imagination of railway photographers and I received many photographs for consideration in this title. Obviously, I could not use them all but, I have reproduced nine photographs in recognition of the special affiliation the photographer had with this tour and the Class 50 locomotive, in particular.

A Class 31 locomotive also featured between Ilkley and Bradford Forster Square, to enable our Class 50 to be released at Ilkley. This locomotive, 31463, is seen passing Bouldon *(right)* en-route to Bradford Forster Square. The other photograph shows 50020 approaching Sheffield *(bottom)* earlier in the day.

both Gavin Morrison

After picking up the last of our passengers at Sheffield, we headed towards Huddersfield, deviating from the main line at Wincobank Station Junction and travelling via Barnsley and Penistone. On this stretch of line, 50020 is first seen at Barnsley Junction, Penistone *(above)* and then later crossing Longroyd Bridge, Huddersfield *(below)*, prior to joining the Trans-Pennine mainline at Springwood Junction.

Two further photographs show 50020 passing through a densely wooded area near Calverley *(right upper)* and, about an hour earlier, heading towards Mirfield *(right lower)*, having passed Heaton Lodge Junction, visible in the background.

Gavin Morrison (2)/N.E. Stead (2)

The 'Skipton Skipper' traversed all three lines which form the 'Shipley triangle' bounded by Bingley, Bradford and Guiseley Junctions, during the day. With the signalman having given us the 'right-away', 500.. is seen leaving Shipley at Bingley Junction (top), on the final leg of the outward journey to Skipton.

When the tour left Bristol in the morning, we could not, unfortunately, provide full catering facilities as our designated restaurant car had been placed in another set of stock. However, undaunted by this, B.R. arranged for the restaurant car to be hauled to Leeds so that hot meals, drinks and snacks could be provided on the return journey.
The stock was split in Leeds City station (middle) so the restaurant car could be added.

Finally, to complete coverage of the 'Skipton Skipper', I have included a photograph of 50020 leaving Bradford Forster Square (bottom), which clearly shows the extent of rationalisation in track and platforms during recent years.

Peter Marsh (2)/A.J. Wood

November 28th: NORFOLKMAN

If ever there was an ill-fated charter, then it had to be the 'Norfolkman'. It was originally planned for May 30th; postponed until October 3rd and then postponed again until November 28th. Even this date posed problems. Firstly, B.R. confirmed that only a single 37/4 locomotive could be provided, when 2×37/4's had been requested and advertised. Secondly, a delicate balancing act of timing had to be carried out to: *(i)* re-route the tour and avoid an engineering blockade between Ely and Norwich, *(ii)* ensure a minimum amount of time for optional activities in Norfolk and *(iii)* ensure getting back beyond Birmingham before engineering works stopped that!

The 'Norfolkman' travelled across Central England and East Anglia to Norwich and Great Yarmouth, with an optional journey along the North Elmham freight branch or a visit to the North Norfolk Railway. It is suffice to say that we experienced further problems on the day, causing the train to arrive significantly late back at Bristol in the evening. The photographs show 37219 *(above)* at Great Yarmouth on the return journey to Norwich and 37428 *(below)*, the main tour engine, at Ipswich station.   *both Norman Preedy*

1988

January 2nd:
KENT COUNTY CRUSADER

At a time when bank holidays come thick and fast and people look for an excuse to get out, we presented the 'Kent County Crusader' – a feast of interesting route and motive power. This was the first tour of 1988 but, in fact, represented the last tour of our 1987 programme.

The tour was based around the use of two Class 33's from Victoria right round to Redhill, plus a Class 73 locomotive (Eastbourne–Brighton) and a Class 50, from and back to Taunton). We headed for the coastline of South East England, traversing lines which normally do not see regular loco. hauled services.

At Victoria, we changed locomotives and 33008 + 33209 (left upper) took over from 50034 (left lower) for the 104 mile journey to Dover Priory. Here, the 'Cromptons' were coupled 'top n' tail' for the trip down the Folkestone Harbour branch and 33209 (top) is seen waiting to depart from Folkestone Harbour. The other photographs show 73138 (middle) at Brighton after arrival from Eastbourne and 50034 (bottom) at Redhill, ready to work home to Taunton.

Steve Turner (3)/Norman Preedy/John Petley

January 30th: FELLSMAN

The Settle & Carlisle Railway is excitedly described as the grandest and most majestic main line in England and this was our destination on the 'Fellsman', being hauled by, not one but, two, of B.R.'s most powerful passenger diesel locomotive – the Class 50. The thought of a pair of Class 50's over Shap and Ais Gill really captured the imagination of people – so much so, that we had to run a relief – 'Fellsman 2' on April 23rd.

Despite a slight 'hiccup' at Gloucester in the morning, when 50034 substituted for 50036, out two 'fifties' (50034 + 50008) performed excellently. The photographic contributions on these two pages reflect the outward and return journeys.

50034 + 50008 are seen passing the village of Tebay *(left upper)* at the commencement of the 5½ mile climb to Shap Summit and about halfway up the climb they were photographed passing Greenholme *(left lower)*. After reversal at Carlisle, we headed home via the S. & C. and 50008 + 50034 are seen slowing down for a photo-stop at Ribblehead *(above)*, after crossing Batty Moss viaduct, and at Long Preston *(below)* between Settle Junction and Hellifield.

B.G. Hughes/ Gavin Morrison (3)

February 27th: PEMBROKE COAST EXPRESS

We thought our 'Peak' tour of last October would mark the end of this respected class but now, in 1988, a handful of examples bravely soldiered on. Therefore, we took the opportunity to add this tour to our programme, giving over 500 'Peak' miles during the day and at the same time taking the class to pastures new – West Wales. The highlight of the route was travel over the Fishguard Harbour and graded Pembroke Dock branches, plus the Trecwn freight branch. As an option, passengers could make a visit to the Gwili Railway instead of traversing the Pembroke Dock branch.

45110 worked from Derby to Llandeilo Junction, where 37428 *(above)* came on for the Llandeilo Junction–Pembroke Dock–Whitland and Letterston Junction–Trecwn sections of the tour. After refuelling, the 'Peak' took us forward from Whitland to Fishguard and 45110 *(below)* is seen waiting to leave Fishguard Harbour and the long run back to Derby. *both Norman Preedy*

March 12th: PENNINE FORTY FAREWELL

The 'Pennine Forty Farewell' represented our last chance to feature stalwart Class 40, D200, at the head of a Pathfinder train on the main line. We devised a special, representative, route that incorporated lines which the Class 40 had been especially associated with over the past 30 years, particularly, the West Coast Main Line and Trans-Pennine routes. An 'Ethel' had to accompany the train to ensure we had warm coaches and we hoped the tour would enable our passengers to say a fond farewell to the 'Green Machine'. Well, this is how the story unfolded. . . .

. . . . the first stretch of the journey was from Taunton to Euston, where we would pick up the Class 40. Over this section, 50001 was diagrammed to work the train and is seen at Queen's Park *(above)*, passing our replacement loco.'s, and at Euston *(below)* upon arrival.

Brian Beer/Bert Wynn

D200 was to be given a fresh coat of paint in readiness for the 'farewell' tours. Unfortunately, this was not completed in time for the March 12 charter but, nevertheless, who would have expected D200 to be turned out in shabby, grey primer paint! However, D200 + Ethel 3 were attached to our train at Euston *(above)* and we departed for the North; seen passing Queens Park *(below)*, 4 miles out of Euston.

Not long out of London, we soon realised that something was wrong with D200 because the train was not gaining any speed – merely dawdling around 45 m.p.h. The train driver telephoned 'control' to advise them of the problem and by the time we reached Stoke, running very late, an assisting engine was waiting to take the train forward. *Norman Preedy/Brian Beer*

At Stoke, 47332 was attached and a fitter came aboard to travel with D200 to see if the 'field divert' electrical fault, which caused the engine to cut out at 50 m.p.h., could be rectified.

At Stockport *(above)*, we were told that the fault could not be fixed and we could either continue 47 hauled (minus D200 + Ethel) or proceed with D200, knowing it would be at reduced speed. We decided to stay with the 'forty' because we felt it important to complete a final run behind a 'whistler' over the Calder Valley and Diggle routes. However, we had to omit Liverpool so passengers could still make their train connections at Birmingham to get home. D200 completed its run over the Pennines and is seen at Horbury *(below)*, near Healey Mills.

This tour may have been an anti-climax for many people but, the 'Pennine Forty Farewell' was unique, in that it has the distinction of being the only charter train to be worked by a Class 40 locomotive, turned out in grey-primer paint!   *Steven Turner/Gavin Morrison*

April 9th: MORECAMBE BAY MARAUDER

This tour was one that had wide appeal, featuring an interesting route around the North-West, including several non-passenger sections (such as Crewe Independent lines, St. Helen's, the Hellifield–Blackburn line) and a journey over the Morecambe–Heysham Harbour branch, all with Class 37 haulage – most unusual for the area! We also included two options for those passengers who wished a break from rail travel during the day – a cruise on Lake Windermere and a visit to the Lakeside & Haverthwaite Steam Railway.

The photographs show 31200 + 31324 *(above)* leaving Morecambe bound for Heysham and 37426 *(below)* departing from Heysham Harbour en route Barrow.
A.J. Woof / Peter Hill

The 'Morecambe Bay Marauder' left Barrow for it's next scheduled stop at Hellifield (photostop). 37426 is seen heading over Kents Viaduct *(above)*, which spans the River Kent estuary near Arnside, and at Carnforth East Junction *(below)*, having traversed the freight-only stretch between Carnforth Furness & Midland and East Junctions.

We re-joined the W.C.M.L. at Farington Junction and proceeded south until 37426 unexpectedly came to a stop at Winwick Junction. In fact, a lump of concrete, which had been suspended over the line by some mindless person, smashed through the centre cab window, fortunately missing the driver but, nevertheless, leaving him very shaken. The train proceeded to Warrington where our driver was taken home and 47553 attached to go forward to Crewe. At Crewe, 31202 replaced 47553 + 37426 for the remainder of the journey home.

A.J. Woof/Peter Hill

April 23rd: FELLSMAN 2

For this 'overspill' tour, an identical route to that of January 30th was chosen but, on this occasion, featuring 50050 + 50024; thus, taking the original 'D400' back to its former stomping grounds. Unfortunately, 50024 suffered 'loss of power' and resulted in 50050 becoming the main train engine between Gloucester-Carlisle-Taunton.

The 'fifties' are seen passing Whitley Crossing *(above)*, north of Wigan, heading down the W.C.M.L. en-route to Carlisle and during a photostop at Ribblehead *(below)*, with Whernside Fell forming the backdrop. Further south, two contrasting photographs show 50024 + 50050 nicely framed by an overbridge at Oakenshaw, Wakefield, *(right upper)* heading towards Hare Park Junction and a high level view *(right lower)* depicting the train as it heads south past Canklow (Rotherham). *Peter Hill/Bert Wynn and Peter Marsh/Gavin Morrison*

April 30th:
CHILTERNIAN

Pathfinder had had little involvement with the magic of main line steam and we felt it was time to put the matter right. The 'Chilternian' was our first main line steam tour, with over 200 miles of steam haulage behind Great Western designed 4-6-0 'Castle' class locomotive, no. 7029 'Clun Castle', all the way from Birmingham to London Marylebone and back.

The 'Chilternian' left Swindon behind 50015 and after picking up our last passengers at Birmingham New Street, we proceeded to Tyseley sidings, where our 'fifty' handed over to 'Clun Castle'. The outward journey is depicted (opposite) and we see 'Clun Castle' with a full head of steam passing through Harbury Cutting (left upper) and at Marylebone (left lower) on arrival.

Whilst the 'Castle' was being 'turned' at Marylebone, there was plenty of opportunity for passengers to take photographs of the locomotive and two photographs (top/middle) have been reproduced to show this.

At Banbury (bottom), on the return journey, 'Clun Castle' took on water and a new train crew for the run to Tyseley. From there we had a storming run, with 'Clun Castle' illuminating the sky with an orange hue as we climbed Hatton Bank – a marvellous sight for any onlooker!

Stever Turner/Norman Preedy (4)

May 14th: PEAK N' SEA

With the extended life of the 'Peak' class locomotives, it proved possible to include an extra tour in our programme, featuring haulage behind an 'O' variant of the Class instead of an e.t.h. one. A circular route was involved from, and back to, Birmingham and after picking up 45052 at Leicester, we set off for our first destination – the Spa Town of Buxton, gained via the interesting and steeply graded branch line from Stockport.

After a break in Buxton, we departed for our second destination, Blackpool, via the new Windsor Link in the Manchester area, two days before it officially opened! The 'Peak N' Sea', with 45052 in charge, is seen traversing the Windsor Link *(above)* and passing Kirkham *(below)* en-route to the seaside resort.

Peter Hill/A.J. Woof

A further two photographs show 45052 on the outskirts of Blackpool at Poulton *(above)* and reversing the stock out of Blackpool North *(below)* in readiness for the return journey. The way home from Blackpool to the Midlands was via Chester, Wrexham and Shrewsbury to give a more scenic and unusual way to end the day.

B.G. Hughes/Stever Turner

May 29th:
CYMRU COLLIER

May was traditionally the month when we enjoyed an entertaining day amongst the hills and valley's of South Wales. 1988 was no exception and we presented a two-pronged attack of the urban Rhondda Vale (Treherbert) and sinuous Cynon Valley (Hirwaun), the latter being one of the longest branch lines in the area, climbing up to meet the Brecon Beacons and Mynydd-Y-Glog, in particular. We also traversed the industrial Uskmouth branch, east of Newport, to conclude the highlights of the day.

Motive Power for the day featured two Class 31's (31155 + 31118) plus a couple of Class 37's (37694 and 37284) to assist over the branch lines.

The photographs depict the three destinations and the motive power involved: 31155 & 31118 on arrival at Treherbert *(top)*, 37694 at Hirwaun *(middle)* and, finally, 37284 at Uskmouth *(bottom)*.

John Chalcraft/Steve Turner/Norman Preedy

June 10-12th: CALEDONIAN

During this weekend, we presented our annual trip to Scotland and the splendour of the Highlands, ranging from the wilds of Caithness and the rolling hills of Banffshire to the tumbling waters of the Spey. When the 'Caledonian' was advertised, we planned to feature: *(i)* 2 × Class 26 locomotives as main motive power, *(ii)* a journey from Inverness to Edinburgh via Aberdeen and *(iii)* a return steam run from Edinburgh to Perth behind 'Black Five' 4-6-0 no. 5305. Disappointingly, late in the day, B.R. informed us that all three aspects could not take place for a variety of reasons.

Main motive power in Scotland for the Mossend–Inverness–Polmadie section turned out to be a pair of Class 37 locomotives, (37035 + 37245) and these are seen on the Highland Line on the climb to Druimuachdar Summit *(above)* and at the Summit itself *(below)*, 1,484 ft. above sea level.

both Gavin Morrison

Before arriving at Inverness, we had the opportunity for a photostop at Kingussie, as we had to wait there to allow a southbound passenger service to pass. 37035 + 37245 are seen at Kingussie *(above)*, sporting one of the two headboards we had made for each portion of the train (see *right upper* for the other headboard).

At Inverness, the train was split into two portions: Portion One for Wick/Thurso and an optional coach trip to John O'Groats and Portion Two for traversal of the Dufftown branch line plus an optional visit to the Glenfiddich Distillery. Portion One is seen leaving Inverness *(below)* with 37416 in charge for the return trip to Wick & Thurso.

Bert Wynn/Steve Turner

The locomotive entrusted to work Portion 2 (Dufftown visit) was Inverness based 37261 and this is seen at Keith *(above)*, with the line to Dufftown seen deviating off to the right of the photograph.

Overnight, the combined train left Inverness for Polmadie, where 37035 + 37245 handed over to 37059 for the journey to Carlisle, via the ex-G.S.W. route. At Carlisle, 47284 came on and we headed for the S. & C. The train was delayed at Kirkby Stephen for about 1 hour because we could not proceed until a safety inspection of Rise Hill Tunnel had been carried out, following a seapage of water through the roof of the tunnel. The 'Caledonian' is seen passing Ribblehead *(below)* with the famous Ribblehead Viaduct and prominent Whernside Fell visible in the background.

Stever Turner/A.J. Woof

July 3rd:
SUFFOLKMAN

The rural East Suffolk line does not see loco-
hauled scheduled services but, the 'Suffolkman'
was to put that right by making a journey from
Ipswich to Lowestoft, headed by a radio-signal-
fitted Class 37. The other interesting parts of the
itinerary included East Anglia bisected by a
Class 50 hauled charter, much of it for the first
time by a 'Fifty'. En-route we travelled via the
W.C.M.L. to London.

The tour got off to a bizarre start. Due to
staffing problems, the e.c.s. for our charter
could not reach Bristol in time and so waited at
Gloucester for a d.m.u. to bring passengers up
from Bristol T.M. and Parkway!

Our 'Fifty', 50022, was photographed at
Goodmayes *(top)* on its trip down the G.E.
mainline and stabled at Ipswich *(bottom)*, where
it came off to allow 37144 to make the journey
to Lowestoft.　　　*Brian Beer/John Chalcraft*

As an option to travelling over the East Suffolk line, passengers could take a special road coach and visit Bressingham Gardens and Steam Museum, by alighting at Ipswich and re-joining the train at Thetford.

We left Ipswich behind 37144 bound for Lowestoft and Norwich and the train is seen at Woodbridge *(above)* and at Lowestoft *(below)*. From Norwich, 50022 hauled the 'Suffolkman' back to Bristol taking in the freight only line in London between Freight Terminal Junction and Camden Road East Junction on the way.

Bert Wynn/Norman Preedy

On the sign in the image:

Rhaid i deithwyr
beidio â chroesi'r
cledrau

Passengers
must not cross
the line

July 17th: CONWAY CRUSADER

This tour featured a class 45/0 locomotive (45012) as main motive power for a visit to Llandudno, Blaenau Ffestiniog and Holyhead. As an option to travelling to Holyhead, passengers could leave the tour at Blaenau Ffestiniog and take the steam train to Porthmadog and then travel by coach through Snowdonia and rejoin the tour at Bangor.

Due to diesel fumes filling one cab end, 45012 was declared a partial failure at Llandudno and 47238 was attached for the run to Blaenau Ffestiniog. However, the climb to the 'Slate Capital' proved too much for 47238 and there was no alternative but for 45012 to provide power from Pont-Y-Pant onwards.

We see 47238 + 45012 ready to leave Llandudno *(above)* and upon arrival at Blaenau Ffestiniog *(right upper)*. 47238 towed 45012 and our train to Holyhead, where 'B.R. Control' confirmed 45012 would work unassisted to Crewe, where 45103 would take over for the run to Birmingham. The 'Conway Crusader' is seen at Holyhead *(right lower)* with 45012 in charge of the last passenger train ever to be worked by a Class 45/0 locomotive on B.R.

Stever Turner (2)/Norman Preedy

August 7th: YORKSHIRE VENTURER

The 'Yorkshire Venturer' proved to be one of the most popular Pathfinder charters ever, giving passengers the opportunity to ride behind 9F Class 2-10-0 no. 92220 'Evening Star'. By also including a Class 50 locomotive, this meant the last passenger rated diesel locomotive and the last steam locomotive to be built by B.R., would both feature on the same tour!

On arrival at York on the outward journey 50037 *(above)* handed over to 92220 'Evening Star' *(below)* for the run to Scarborough and Hull.

both Bert Wynn

On a glorious summer's day, passengers enjoyed the splendour of steam behind 'Evening Star', especially remembered for her days on the 'Somerset & Dorset' in the early 'sixties. The two photographs show her at a photostop at Bridlington *(top)* and at Scarborough *(middle)*, waiting to be reversed on the turntable for the run to Hull.

On arrival at Hull Paragon station, 'Evening Star' was detached so 50037 could take the train forward, having earlier run light engine from York. The 'Yorkshire Venturer', with 50037 in charge, is seen at Gilberdyke *(bottom)* homeward bound.

Bert Wynn/Norman Preedy/P. Watson

August 20th:
PATHFINDER SCOT

The 'Pathfinder Scot' was a special train from th[e]
Mid-West, Severnside and Midlands via the We[st]
Coast Main Line to Edinburgh. At our destinatio[n]
passengers had the choice of spending five hou[rs]
at their leisure or selecting an optional activity —
Firth of Forth boat cruise, coach tour of Edinbur[gh]
and its Castle, the Bo'ness Railway or a visit [to]
selective B.R. Depots'.

Following the withdrawal of the remaining 'Pea[k]
locomotives, motive power was 45106, the ne[w]
celebrity locomotive, which had been retained [by]
B.R., primarily for charter work. This wa[s]
45106's first passenger working since being ove[r-]
haulled (D Exam) and re-painted in green live[ry]
by members of Tinsley (Sheffield) t.m.d. staff[.]

The impressive buildings and castle dominate th[e]
Edinburgh skyline in the aerial photograp[h]
which shows 45106 (left) taking the e.c.s. [to]
Craigentinny for servicing following arrival [at]
Waverley station. After an enjoyable day, pas[s-]
engers re-joined the 'Pathfinder Scot' and wait[ed]
for 45106 (bottom), looking in pristine conditio[n]
to leave Edinburgh.   both Steve Turn[er]

September 10th:
TYNESIDER

The 'Tynesider' was a repeat of the visit we made to the North East on August 22nd 1987 but, this time, featuring green-liveried, Petroleum Sector, 37350 (D6700) as motive power and travel to/from Newcastle via the E.C.M.L. There were also optional activities to choose from, viz: (i) coach trip to the North of England Open Air Museum at Beamish, (ii) the Tyne & Wear Metro system in Newcastle or, (iii) coach trip to B.R. installations at Blyth, Gateshead, Sunderland and Thornaby.

From Newcastle, the tour traversed the freight only/diversionary route via Benton Quarry Junction and Bedlington Junction, before rejoining the E.C.M.L. at Morpeth. An aerial photograph shows 37350 leaving Newcastle *(right)* bound for Morpeth and at Clay Cross *(bottom)*, south of Chesterfield, on the outward journey.

Steve Turner/Gavin Morrison

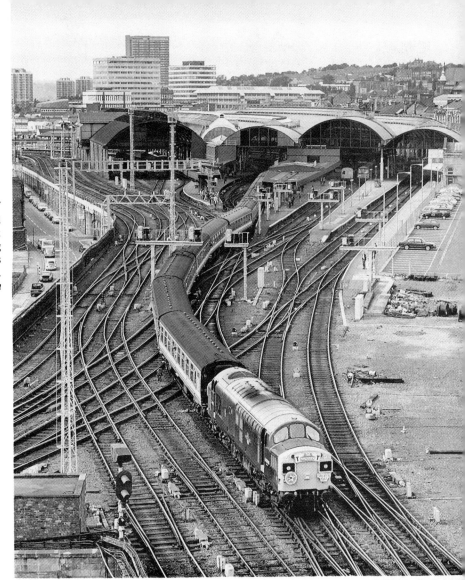

October 22nd: PENNINE FIFTIES

Following the success of the 'Fellsman', we received many requests to organise a 'fifty' hauled charter to Liverpool, taking in the E.C.M.L. and a trans-pennine crossing. Well, the 'Pennine Fifties' was the result, featuring 2 × Class 50 locomotives.

However, prior to this tour, B.R. had confirmed that Class 50s' would not be allowed to work charter trains in the future, due to their poor performance record. Luckily, with special B.R. dispensation, the 'Pennine Fifties' was allowed to run 'fifty' hauled.

An interesting route was chosen, including lines unusual for loco. hauled trains, such as the Bradford (Wilts) North Chord, Haringay Curve (London) and the Hertford Loop, plus a run down the E.C.M.L. and a pennine crossing over the Diggle route to Liverpool. Motive power was 50033 + 50034 and the pair are seen at Bradford North Junction *(above)* and at Crewe *(below)*, on the outward and return journey, respectively.

P. Strong/B.G. Hughes

November 5th: WESSEX ADVENTURER

As a result of public demand, we started this tour from Manchester to give people living in the North-West a chance to sample a Pathfinder tour and enjoy an interesting day out by train. The sole remaining 'Peak', 45106, was requested as motive power to haul the train deep into Southern territory, featuring travel over two differing branch lines – the 'oil line' to Fawley and the Weymouth Quay tramline. Two Class 33 locomotives also performed during the day.

The Eastleigh depot loop had been requested but, due to operational difficulties, could not be traversed and the train was routed via a freight line through Millbrook Freightliner Terminal instead. The 'Wessex Adventurer' is seen passing Northam Junction *(above)*, near Southampton, with 45106 in charge, en-route to Fawley. Traversal of the Weymouth Quay tramline required 'top n' tail' 'cromptons' (33102 + 33114) and 33102 is seen at Weymouth Quay *(below)* prior to departure.   *B.G. Hughes/Steve Turner*

November 19th: LINCOLN SHIRE RAMBLER

As Class 50 locomotives were no longer allowed to work charters, motive power for this charter was changed to 45106. This was a great disappointment as the itinerary had been especially chosen with a Class 50 in mind. However, our circular route centred on the county of Lincolnshire, with a visit to Skegness, out of season, then moving onto Humberside for freight line travel over the Immingham Loop, followed by a journey over the freight-only South Yorkshire Joint Line. Unfortunately, due to late running, we traversed the latter line in darkness.

The pictorial record of the 'Lincoln Shire Rambler' is at Skegness, showing 45106 *(above)* shunting the stock into a siding for 'run-round' purposes and 45106 *(below)* awaiting departure time from the holiday resort. *Steve Turner/Bert Wynn*

"THE EXECUTIVES"

October 1st:
PENNINE EXECUTIVE

December 3rd:
FESTIVE PENNINE EXECUTIVE

We decided to launch a new programme of Luxury Dining Landcruises to provide future growth for the Company. Each train carries an 'Executive' name to reflect quality and personal service. The carriages are all first class and air-conditioned, with a full 'at seat' meal service consisting of 'The Great English Cooked Breakfast', Light Luncheon and Evening Dinner included in the fare. Each 'Executive' features travel over scenic routes and to interesting destinations.

The first dining landcruise ran on October 1st to Carlisle and Appleby, featuring a southbound run over the 'threatened with closure' Settle & Carlisle route. Unfortunately, we experienced many operational problems on the day, which resulted in B.R. laying on a 'without charge' re-run for our passengers.

The 'Festive Pennine Executive' was a repeat of October 1st but this time making a northbound run over the S. & C. for a mid-day break at Carlisle instead. This train, hauled by 47611, is seen passing Longbridge *(top)* and during a photostop at Garsdale *(bottom)*, on the outward journey. An additional photograph *(middle)* has been included to show the typical table layout inside a coach on which the meals are served. *Peter Tandy/Martin Buck (2)*

GLOSSARY

1. Schedule of Special Trains.

The following is a complete list of all the special trains run by *Pathfinder Tours* during 1987 and 1988, inclusive of the locomotives featured.

1987

March 7th CUMBRIAN MOUNTAINEER
1Z36 Plymouth - Carlisle

47597	Plymouth	– Bristol T.M.
* 45120	Bristol T.M.	– Derby
45119	Derby	– Carlisle
45119	Carlisle	– Bristol T.M.
31406/465	Bristol T.M.	– Plymouth

* Loco. failed

March 21st YORKSHIRE ROSE
1Z36 Cardiff Central - York

37430	Cardiff Central	– York
37430	York	– Cardiff Central

April 18th TAMAR-FORTH EXPRESS
1Z26 Plymouth - Edinburgh

50030	Plymouth	– Birmingham N. St.
* 81020	Birmingham N. St.	– Carnforth
47258	Carnforth	– Carlisle
81004	Carlisle	– Carstairs
26032/043	Carstairs	– Edinburgh
26032/043	Edinburgh	– Carstairs
81006	Carstairs	– Birmingham N. St.
47609	Birmingham	– Plymouth

* Loco. failed

May 3rd HASTINGS BELLE
1Z36 Bristol T.M. - Eastbourne

56033	Bristol T.M.	– Victoria
33029	Victoria	– East Grinstead
33029	East Grinstead	– Norwood Jct.
56033	Norwood Jct.	– Eastbourne
73132	Eastbourne	– Hastings
56033	Hastings	– Paddington
56048	Paddington	– Bristol T.M.

May 23rd GWENT VALLEY EXPLORER
1Z37 Crewe - Barry Island

40122	Crewe	– Waunllwyd
37280	Waunllwyd	– Newport
37220	Newport	– Machen
37280	Machen	– Barry Island
37280	Barry Island	– Cardiff Central
40122	Cardiff Central	– Oakdale
40122	Oakdale	– Crewe

May 31st BARMOUTH BAY EXPRESS
1Z27 Bristol T.M. - Machynlleth
1L40 Machynlleth - Barmouth

37159/204	Bristol T.M.	– Machynlleth
* 7819	Machynlleth	– Barmouth
* 7819	Barmouth	– Machynlleth
37159/204	Machynlleth	– Bristol T.M.

* 'Manor' Class 4-6-0 'Hinton Manor'

June 27th AINTREE HURDLER
1Z27 Bristol T.M. - Aintree

47564	Bristol T.M.	– Shrewsbury
58042	Shrewsbury	– Liverpool L. St.
58042	Liverpool L. St.	– Aintree
58042	Aintree	– Toton
58031	Toton	– Birmingham N. St.
47590	Birmingham N. St.	– Bristol T.M.

July 12th WELSH RAMBLER
1Z36 Leicester - Carmarthen

20021/113	Leicester	– Margam
37162	Margam	– Swansea
20021/113	Swansea	– Carmarthen
20021/113	Carmarthen	– Birmingham N. St.
37693	Birmingham N. St.	– Gloucester

July 25th HUMBERMAN
1Z36 Exeter St. D. - Cleethorpes

50024	Exeter St. D.	– Bristol T.M.
37699/139	Bristol T.M.	– Barnetby
47222	Barnetby	– Cleethorpes
37699/139	Cleethorpes	– Bristol T.M.
47513	Bristol T.M.	– Exeter St. D.

August 9th RHEIDOL RAMBLER
1Z26 Bristol T.M. - Aberystwyth

47587	Bristol T.M.	– Wolverhampton
20133/034	Wolverhampton	– Aberystwyth
20133/034	Aberystwyth	– Wolverhampton
47453	Wolverhampton	– Bristol T.M.

August 22nd NORTHUMBRIAN
1Z38 Swindon - Newcastle

50001	Swindon	– Birmingham N. St.
56016	Birmingham N. St.	– Carlisle
37180	Carlisle	– Newcastle
56005	Newcastle	– Morpeth
56005	Morpeth	– Ryhope Grange
56005	Ryhope Grange	– Newcastle
37180	Newcastle	– Carlisle
56016	Carlisle	– Birmingham N. St.
47478	Birmingham N. St.	– Swindon

September 18th–20th SON O SKIRL
1Z27 Bristol T.M. - Fort William
1Z55 Fort William - Mallaig
1Z56 Mallaig - Fort William
1L00 Manchester V - Southport

50005	Bristol T.M.	– Birmingham N. St.
81009	Birmingham N. St.	– Carlisle
40122 + 'Ethel'	Carlisle	– Mossend
37092/043	Mossend	– Fort William
* { 2005	Fort William	– Mallaig
{ 2005	Mallaig	– Fort William
37092/043	Fort William	– Glasgow Cent.
81009	Glasgow Cent.	– Polmadie
40122 + 'Ethel'	Polmadie	– Manchester V.
** 4472	Manchester V.	– Southport
*** 20052/104	Southport	– Bescot
20154/197	Bescot	– Gloucester
47381	Gloucester	– Bristol T.M.

* 'K1' Class 2-6-0
** 'A3' Class 4-6-2 'Flying Scotsman'
*** 20104 failed at Penkridge

October 3rd 45 FINALE
1Z46 Bristol T.M. - Scarborough

45106	Bristol T.M.	– Birmingham N. St.
* 45007/106	Birmingham N. St.	– Leicester
45007/107	Leicester	– Scarborough
45007/107	Scarborough	– Hull
45007/107	Hull	– Birmingham N. St.
45107	Birmingham N. St.	– Bristol T.M.

* 45106 failed en route

October 17th BLACKPOOL ILLUMINATOR
1Z47 Bristol T.M. - Blackpool North

47625	Bristol T.M.	– Blackpool North
* 37901	Bromsgrove	– Blackwell
47625	Blackpool North	– Bristol T.M.

* assist 1Z47

October 31st SEVERN-CLYDE EXPRESS
1Z38 Bristol T.M. - Glasgow Central

47465	Bristol T.M.	– Birmingham N. St.
87029	Birmingham N. St.	– Carlisle
47653	Carlisle	– Glasgow Cent.
20205/217	Glasgow Cent.	– Carstairs
81011	Carstairs	– Birmingham N. St.
47561	Birmingham N. St.	– Bristol T.M.

November 14th SKIPTON SKIPPER
1Z25 Bristol T.M. - Skipton

50020	Bristol T.M.	– Ilkley
31463	Ilkley	– Bradford F. Sq.
50020	Bradford F. Sq.	– Skipton
50020	Skipton	– Bristol T.M.

November 28th NORFOLKMAN
1Z27 Bristol T.M. - Great Yarmouth

37428	Bristol T.M.	– Norwich
37219	Norwich	– Gt. Yarmouth
37219	Gt. Yarmouth	– Norwich
37428	Norwich	– Bristol T.M.

1988

January 2nd KENT COUNTY CRUSADER
1Z26 Taunton - Folkestone Harbour

50034	Taunton	– Victoria
33008/209	Victoria	– Dover Priory
33209	Dover Priory	– Folkestone Hbr.
33008	Folkestone Hbr.	– Folkestone East
33209	Folkestone East	– Ashford
33209/008	Ashford	– Eastbourne
73138	Eastbourne	– Brighton
33008/209	Brighton	– Redhill
50034	Redhill	– Taunton

January 30th FELLSMAN
1Z26 Taunton - Carlisle

* 50008/036	Taunton	– Gloucester
50034/008	Gloucester	– Carlisle
50034/0008	Carlisle	– Gloucester
50036	Gloucester	– Taunton

* 50036 failed at Gloucester

February 27th PEMBROKE COAST EXPLORER
1Z27 Derby - Fishguard Harbour

45110	Derby	– Llandeilo Jct.
37428	Llandeilo Jct.	– Pembroke Dock
37428	Pembroke Dock	– Whitland
45110	Whitland	– Letterston Jct.
37428	Letterston Jct.	– Trecwn
45110	Trecwn	– Fishguard Hbr.
45110	Fishguard Hbr	– Derby

March 12th PENNINE FORTY FAREWELL
1Z36 Taunton - Liverpool L. St.

50001	Taunton	– Euston
40122 + 'Ethel'	Euston	– Stoke
* 47332	Stoke	– Stockport
40122 + 'Ethel'	Stockport	– Crewe
85008	Crewe	– Birmingham N. St.
47575	Birmingham N. St.	– Gloucester
50029	Gloucester	– Taunton

* Assisting 40122 + 'Ethel'

April 1st/2nd BALLIGO DIVIDER
B979 Bray - Mullingar - (B980 return)
B879 Mullingar - Claremorris - (B880 return)
B881 Claremorris - Ballina - (B882 return)
A908 Mullingar - Sligo

009	Bray	– Dublin
056	Dublin	– Claremorris
123/127	Mullingar	– Sligo
123/127	Sligo	– Ballina
E428	Claremorris	– Ballina
E428	Ballina	– Claremorris
056	Claremorris	– Bray

April 9th MORECAMBE BAY MARAUDER
1Z16 Taunton - Barrow In Furness

37426	Taunton	– Morecambe
* 37059	Bromsgrove	– Blackwell
31200/324	Morecambe	– Heysham
37426	Heysham	– Morecambe
31200/324	Morecambe	– Barrow I. F.
37426	Barrow I. F.	– Warrington B. Q.
** 47553	Warrington B. Q.	– Crewe
31202	Crewe	– Taunton

* assist 1Z16
** replaced 37426 due to broken cab window

April 23rd FELLSMAN 2
1Z41 Taunton - Carlisle

50050/024	Taunton	– Gloucester
* 50050/024	Gloucester	– Carlisle
50050/024	Carlisle	– Taunton

* 50024 did not provide power Gloucester-Carlisle-Taunton

April 30th CHILTERNIAN
1Z40 Swindon - Marylebone

50015	Swindon	– Tyesley
* 7029	Tyseley	– Marylebone
7029	Marylebone	– Tyesley
50015	Tyseley	– Bristol T.M.
47624	Bristol T.M.	– Swindon

* 'Castle' Class 4-6-0 'Clun Castle'

May 14th PEAK 'N' SEA
1Z42 Swindon - Blackpool North

47450	Swindon	– Birmingham N. St.
45110	Birmingham N. St.	– Leicester
45052	Leicester	– Buxton
45052	Buxton	– Blackpool North
45052	Blackpool North	– Birmingham N. St.
47450	Birmingham N. St.	– Swindon

May 29th CYMRU COLLIER
1Z27 Crewe - Hirwaun

31155/118	Crewe	– Treherbert
37694	Treherbert	– Pontypridd
31155/118	Pontypridd	– Hirwaun
37694	Hirwaun	– Cardiff Central
31155/118	Cardiff Central	– Uskmouth
37284	Uskmouth	– Newport
31155/118	Newport	– Crewe

June 10th-12th CALEDONIAN
1Z42 Reading - Inverness
1Z49 Inverness - Wick
1Z51 Inverness - Dufftown
1Z50 Thurso - Inverness
1Z52 Dufftown - Inverness
1Z70 Inverness - Edinburgh
1Z42 Edinburgh - Reading

47497	Reading	– Birmingham N. St.	
85010	Birmingham N. St.	– Mossend	
37035/245	Mossend	– Inverness	
37261	Inverness	– Dufftown	Portion 2
37261	Dufftown	– Inverness	
37416	Inverness	– Wick	Portion 1
37416	Thurso	– Inverness	
37035/245	Inverness	– Polmadie	
37059	Polmadie	– Carlisle	
47284	Carlisle	– Carnforth	
85020	Carnforth	– Birmingham N. St.	
47466	Birmingham N. St.	– Reading	

July 3rd SUFFOLKMAN
1Z37 Bristol T.M. - Norwich

Dmu	Bristol T.M.	– Gloucester
50022	Gloucester	– Ipswich
37144	Ipswich	– Lowestoft
37144	Lowestoft	– Norwich
50022	Norwich	– Bristol T.M.

July 17th CONWAY CRUSADER
1Z43 Reading – Holyhead

50035	Reading	– Birmingham N. St.
*45012	Birmingham N. St.	– Llandudno
**47238/45012	Llandudno	– Blaeneau Ffestiniog
47238	Blaeneau Ffest.	– Holyhead
45012	Holyhead	– Crewe
45103	Crewe	– Birmingham N. St.
50035	Birmingham N. St.	– Reading

* Loco. declared partial failure at Llandudno
** 45012 only provided power Pont-Y-Pant to Blaeneau Ffestiniog

August 7th YORKSHIRE VENTURER
1Z46 Swindon – Scarborough

50037	Swindon	– York
*{92220	York	– Scarborough
{92220	Scarborough	– Hull
50037	Hull	– Swindon

* Class 9F 2-10-0 'Evening Star'

August 20th PATHFINDER SCOT
1Z38 Reading – Edinburgh

50030	Reading	– Birmingham N. St.
45106	Birmingham N. St.	– Edinburgh
45106	Edinburgh	– Birmingham N. St.
50030	Birmingham N. St.	– Reading

September 10th TYNESIDER
1Z36 Reading – Morpeth

37350	Swindon	– Morpeth
37350	Morpeth	– Swindon

October 1st PENNINE EXECUTIVE
(First Luxury Dining Train)
1Z48 Swindon – Carlisle

47654	Swindon	– Carlisle
47654	Carlisle	– Bristol T.M.
47559	Bristol T.M.	– Swindon

October 22nd PENNINE FIFTIES
1Z26 Birmingham N. St. – Liverpool Lime Street

50033/34	Birmingham N. St.	– Bristol T.M.
50033/34	Bristol T.M.	– Liverpool L. St.
50033/34	Liverpool L. St.	– Swindon

November 5th WESSEX ADVENTURER
1Z37 Manchester Picc. – Weymouth Quay

45106	Manchester Picc.	– Fawley
33114/102	Fawley	– Southampton
45106	Southampton	– Bournemouth
33114/102	Bournemouth	– Weymouth
33114/102	Weymouth	– Weymouth Jct.
33114	Weymouth Jct.	– Weymouth Quay
33102	Weymouth Quay	– Weymouth Jct.
*45106	Weymouth Jct.	– Manchester Picc.

* Loco. failed on arrival

November 19th LINCOLN SHIRE RAMBLER
1Z42 Swindon – Skegness

47557	Swindon	– Nottingham
45106	Nottingham	– Skegness
45106	Skegness	– Birmingham N. St.
47637	Birmingham N. St.	– Swindon

November 26th PENNINE EXECUTIVE
(B.R. courtesy Re-Run of October 1st train)
1Z38 Swindon – Carlisle

47661	Swindon	– Carlisle
47661	Carlisle	– Swindon

December 3rd FESTIVE PENNINE EXECUTIVE
1Z47 Swindon – Carlisle

47611	Swindon	– Carlisle
47552	Carlisle	– Bristol T.M.
47468	Bristol T.M.	– Swindon

2. Headboards

It has always been our custom, whenever possible, to display a Pathfinder 'house board' plus a main train headboard on each of our charters. These are kindly made for us by Mark Alden and we would like to acknowledge our thanks to him for this service. A selection of these headboards are shown below, which are self explanatory. *Photographs by Martin Buck*

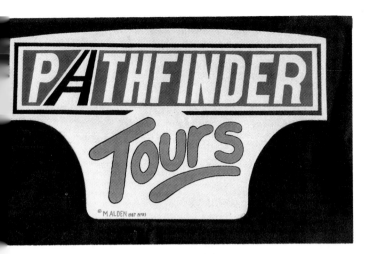

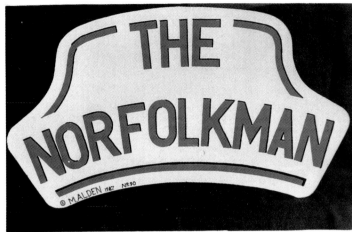

3. Overseas

Pathfinder Tours have only ventured overseas once during 1987/88 – a trip to the Republic of Ireland, although we cannot rule out future ventures, especially to the Continent when the Channel Tunnel is opened.

April 3rd 1988: BALLIGO DIVIDER

After a 3½ hour Irish Sea crossing from Holyhead to Dun-Laoghaire, we joined our special C.I.E. train for the journey to Mullingar. Here, passengers had a choice of either travelling to Ballina and back or, detrain and take a connecting service train to Sligo, thence special road coaches to Ballina, to rejoin the tour.

As an aside, the local churchgoing people at Mullingar were amazed at the number of 'english speaking' people, who were taking breakfast in the various cafes' in the town!

Haulage was not only behind General Motors diesel loco's but also the preserved Maybach engined E428. The photographs show no. 056 (right) and no. E428 (bottom) at Claremorris.

both Bert Wynn